P9-APL-106

NAME YOUR EMOTIONS

SOMETIMES I FEEL WORRIED

by Jaclyn Jaycox

PEBBLE
a capstone imprint

Pebble Emerge is published by Pebble, an imprint of Capstone.
1710 Roe Crest Drive
North Mankato, Minnesota 56003
www.capstonepub.com

Copyright © 2021 by Capstone. All rights reserved. No part of this publication may be reproduced in whole or in part, or stored in a retrieval system, or transmitted in any form or by any means, electronic, mechanical, photocopying, recording, or otherwise, without written permission of the publisher.

Library of Congress Cataloging-in-Publication Data is available on the Library of Congress website.
ISBN 978-1-9771-2465-4 (library binding)
ISBN 978-1-9771-2641-2 (paperback)
ISBN 978-1-9771-2508-8 (eBook PDF)

Summary: What does it mean to feel worried? Everyone feels worried sometimes. Learn how to recognize, name, and manage your emotions. Stunning photos illustrate what being worried looks like. A mindfulness activity will help children learn how to turn worried feelings into good ones!

Image Credits
Capstone Studio: Karon Dubke, 21; Shutterstock: Anatoliy Karlyuk, 7, cheapbooks, 5, Color Symphony, Design Element, DGLimages, 15, Evgeny Hmur, 16, fizkes, 13, Halfpoint, 11, InesBazdar, 19, Jimena Roquero, 17, Kleber Cordeiro, 9, MNStudio, 6, Mongkolchon Akesin, 18, pathdoc, Cover

Editorial Credits
Designer: Kay Fraser; Media Researcher: Tracy Cummins; Production Specialist: Katy LaVigne

All internet sites appearing in back matter were available and accurate when this book was sent to press.

Printed in the United States 4217

TABLE OF CONTENTS

Words in **bold** are in the glossary.

WHAT IS WORRY?

Imagine it's your first day at a new school. You don't know any of the other kids or teachers. How would that make you feel? Chances are you might feel worried.

Worry is an **emotion**, or feeling. Everyone feels worried sometimes. People have lots of different feelings every day.

WHAT DOES IT FEEL LIKE TO BE WORRIED?

Think of a time you felt worried. Maybe you had a big test coming up in school. Maybe someone you love was sick. How did you feel?

When you are worried, your heart beats faster. Your hands get sweaty. You might feel tired but have trouble sleeping. You might even feel sick to your stomach.

USING YOUR SENSES

Everyone has five **senses**. People can touch, taste, see, hear, and smell things. Your senses send messages to your brain. That's where emotions start.

Hearing a noise in your closet at night can make you feel worried. Seeing lightning can make you worry about a storm coming.

TALKING ABOUT YOUR FEELINGS

Sometimes people don't want to let others know they are worried. But it is important to talk about your feelings. Keeping them inside makes you feel worse.

Tell a friend or family member how you are feeling. They may know how to help. Talking about your feelings can make you feel better too.

UNDERSTANDING WORRY

Everyone feels worried at times. Worries can be big or small. It's OK to feel worried. You just don't want it to last too long.

It's important to know what causes your feelings. Then you can figure out what to do to feel better. Worry comes from thinking something bad is going to happen.

Worry can be a strong feeling. It can make learning harder. You can get **distracted**. You might have trouble listening to your teacher.

But worry can also be a helpful feeling. If you didn't worry about your math test, you might not study for it.

HANDLING YOUR FEELINGS

How you handle your feelings matters. You want to deal with them in a healthy way. Talk about your worries. You could even draw a picture of them.

Think about why you are worrying. Is there anything you can do to fix it? If not, try to move on. There are things you can do to feel better.

You can take a deep breath. Go play outside. Try to **relax**. Read your favorite book. Do an art project. Give someone you love a hug.

You can help others that feel worried too. Be a good listener. Tell them you are there for them. Ask if they want to play a game. Try to take their mind off of their worries.

MINDFULNESS ACTIVITY

Let's go on an adventure! We are going to explore the great outdoors. But with a little twist! You must be very quiet. Use your eyes and ears to find things that crawl, fly, or hop.

Do you see a caterpillar crawling up a tree?

Do you see a bee buzzing around a flower?

Now listen. Can you hear birds chirping?

Can you hear a squirrel running through the leaves?

You'll be amazed at what you find in nature when you use your senses.

GLOSSARY

distracted (dis-TRAKT-ed)—to have a hard time focusing on one thing

emotion (i-MOH-shuhn)—a strong feeling; people have and show emotions such as happiness, sadness, fear, anger, and jealousy

relax (ri-LAKS)—to calm down

sense (SENSS)—a way of knowing about your surroundings; hearing, smelling, touching, tasting, and sight are the five senses

READ MORE

Christelis, Paul. *Questions and Feelings About Worries*. North Mankato, MN: Picture Window Books, 2019.

Percival, Tom. *Ruby Finds a Worry*. New York: Bloomsbury, 2019.

INTERNET SITES

Emotions Coloring Pages

coloring.ws/emotion.htm

Kids' Health – Worry Less in 3 Steps

kidshealth.org/en/kids/worry-less.html?ref=search

INDEX